The Parish of Christ Church

Serving at the Altar

FOR USE BY:

THE ALTAR AND SERVERS GUILD

SACRISTANS, SACRISTANS ASSISTANTS, CRUCIFERS, HEAD SERVER, ACOLYTES AND THURIFERS

Contents

Foreword:

If you are reading this Manual, I would like to thank you for your willingness to serve our Lord by assisting the clergy in preparing for the worship of Almighty God. I cannot thank enough all of the faithful Altar Guild members, Sacristans, Sacristans Assistants, Crucifers, Head Server, Acolytes and Thurifers who have served the Parish of Christ Church so faithfully throughout the years. Your faithful service has not only eased a Priest's load, but blessed countless lives with your behind the scenes service of the Lord.

May your service continue to bless us all.

This Altar Manual is meant to be a guide and a help for those seeking to properly prepare the Altar and serve in the various aspects of Anglican worship.

It is not all-inclusive and care should be taken to follow the guidance of your Priest in these areas.

This guide is meant to help things to be done properly and good order:

(1 Corinthians 14:40) But everything must be done in a proper and orderly way.

(Psalm 96:9) Worship the Lord in holy splendour; tremble before him, all the earth!

Altar and Servers Guild Mission, Purpose, and Membership

The Altar Guild is a lay ministry to serve God in His house by preparing the Sanctuary for worship, maintaining and caring for the sacred vessels, altar linens, and vestments, and serving the clergy and the parish. Prior to the nineteenth century, these duties were performed by the clergy and later by the sacristan or parish clerk. By the late nineteenth century, the altar guild had come into being.

The Rector (or Vicar) is the head of the altar guild, which functions under his guidance and direction. The rector appoints the director of the altar guild and its members.

1. Altar Guild members should be congregants confirmed in the Anglican Church and should view their service as a sacred duty.
2. The Servers guild should be Baptised members of the Anglican Church between the ages of six and thirteen years old.

   As written so beautifully by Josephine Smith Wood in her Altar Guild Manual, 1915: "Before entering upon work about the Altar, kneel a few moments at the Chancel rail, and, offering your work to God, ask Him to accept and bless it, and enable you to do it worthily as unto Him. It is a great honour and privilege to be allowed to care for the holy things in God's house, and a devout spirit and reverent demeanour should characterize those who are thus engaged."

Things to keep in mind

- Show up on your scheduled Sunday. People are depending on you for guidance through the worship service. You are an important and vital element to the service.

1. If you cannot avail yourself, call a substitute; CALL the Church Warden on duty with the name of your substitute, if they agree. If you cannot find a substitute or you are not able to serve. CALL the Rector on 062 318 8379. A Sacristan, Crucifer and Acolytes phone list will be placed in the Vestry.

Remember the three P's:

1. **Punctuality** is important. When you arrive on time, everything flows more smoothly. Get to church at least 45 minutes before the service is due to begin; if the service is at 09:00 you must be at the Church by arrive by 08:15.
2. **Pay Attention**. Take a few minutes before the service to familiarize yourself with the order of worship found in an Anglican Prayer Book and the bulletin. This will help you stay on top of things and know where you are in the service so that you will be prepared; it will also help you anticipate any last-minute changes.
   i. Get questions answered early. Ask the lead Acolyte, Deacon or Celebrant (Priest).
   ii. Know who the Altar Guild messenger for the service is and know where they are sitting during the service, in case there is a need for more bread or wine.
   iii. You may want to use a pencil to check off each section of the service to help you follow along. Be flexible, ready for changes, minor changes happen often. Be prepared for surprises, they do happen!
3. **Participate**. Most importantly, don't forget to worship God. That's why we are here! As a leader in the service, you are a role model to others, especially younger children in the congregation.
   i. Work together as a team with the other acolytes, help each other, and look to your head acolyte for direction, head acolytes look to Deacon / Celebrant for direction.
   ii. Move about with dignity, not too fast, not too slow, use purposeful movements. Show reverence to the Altar. If you are doing your best, and moving with dignity, no one will notice mistakes.
   iii. Know your cassock size. Help is always available. You may wear your own Medallion.

iv. If you have trouble with a wick or candle, notify the Altar Guild lay minister on that Sunday. They can help! You can find their name in the service bulletin. Do not try to fix the problem on your own.

v. Remember we are here to serve our Holy Father, Jesus Christ and the Holy Spirit.

What to wear

1. Do not wear:
   - Short pants, knee length pants or very short skirts cut off or torn jeans, tee shirts or shirts with questionable logos or insignias.
   - Always wear clothing which is respectable to the worship of God .
   - Lightweight clothing is suggested, it gets warm in a cassock.
   - Comfortable, respectable shoes or sandals. Don't wear flip flops, shower shoes, slippers beach shoes or tekkies.
   - Sacristans dress in white Alb and black cincture / rope girdle and servers wear a red cassock and a white cincture / rope girdle with a white surplus.

Acolyte's prayer

Said in the vestry after dressing

"Gracious God, You call your servant to light the way for your people in a world of change and uncertainty. Grant to your acolyte reverent heart, steady hands, and the will to persevere in service at your altar and at prayer.

Father, Allow me to show your grace, patience, power, and peace by my service and devotion to you this day and the days ahead.

Bless and guide me by your wisdom and help me to spread your word throughout the world through Jesus Christ our Lord, who lives and reigns with you and the Holy Spirit, one God now and forever. Amen. "

Sacristans and the Servers Guild Training, Responsibilities, Tasks

Altar guild members should receive instruction in 'setting up' for services, removal and cleansing of vessels and linens after the services, names of all the vessels, linens and vestments used in the church, liturgical colours and seasons, use of flowers, use of candles, church symbols, and parts of the church.

In most Anglican churches, altar guild duties include:

1. Making sure that the Sanctuary is dusted and cleaned thoroughly before and after services.
2. Placement of proper seasonal colours, hangings and falls.
3. Preparation of the Altar Table for services.
4. Preparation of the Credence Table/Shelf.
5. Arrangement and placement of fresh flowers (some churches have a flower guild for this).
6. Placement of the candles on the Altar Table and within the Sanctuary.
7. Ensuring that the priest's vestments are cleaned, pressed and hanging in the Sacristy.
8. Care, preparation, cleansing, and storing of all the sacred vessels, linens, hangings, and candles.

Diocesan Guild of Servers members should receive instruction in preparation for service in the procession for services at the altar and in the Chancel, assisting the priest, deacon and lay ministers in performing their duties, names of all the vessels, linens and vestments used in the church, liturgical colours and seasons, use of crucifer, use of Thurible, use of candles, church symbols, and parts of the church.

In most Anglican churches, server's guild duties and rules include:

1. Arrive 30 minutes before the service time. If you're very late you might not receive an assignment.
2. Check for any new materials, either posted or to be passed out.
3. Please, no patterned clothes only black pants or skirt. Shoes should be polished, hands and fingernails clean, and hair properly dressed.
4. Drinks should be left outside the vestry.
5. Follow the service in the Anglican Prayer Book, and bulletin, and make all responses in a clear and audible voice. Be prepared to stay for 5 to 10 minutes after a service for comments and announcements.
6. Inappropriate behaviour will not be tolerated. Please refrain from comments and actions that will detract from focusing on our preparation and service to the Glory of God.
7. Diocesan Guild of Servers serve throughout the year, it is to be noted that during LENT, EASTER TIDE, ADVENT and CHRISTMAS we will require at least a Crucifer, a Thurifer and two Acolytes. Therefore if you are planning to be away from Potchefstroom during any of these days then please inform the priest at least one month in advance so that arrangements may be made.
8. There are weekly training, rehearsing, instruction, examination and Sacristan duties days for these meetings will be communicated to you. Important meetings are on the following days the Saturday before Palm Sunday, Easter Sunday and Christmas.
9. You should be familiar with all Parish serving materials.
10. You're encouraged to know by heart the prayer of S. Vincent, which is said in the Galilee before each service.

Prayer of S. Vincent:

Father God, You see before You a Company that longs only for the grace to observe your teachings, to model itself on Your way of acting and to advance in the ways of holiness You have prescribed for it, in Jesus Christs name we pray, Amen

The Prayer for Diocesan Guild of Servers is to be said before each meeting. Make a copy of this prayer and carry it with you so that you may say it frequently.

The Prayer for Diocesan Guild of Servers Members:

Almighty God, who has called us Your servants to the sacred office of Diocesan Guild of Servers in Your church, that clothed in red and white we may minister before You, we pray Your great mercy to guide, strengthen, and sanctify us by Your Holy Spirit, that, always doing Your will, we may both by our service in Your House and by our daily life, please You and glorify Your Name, through Jesus Christ, our Lord. Amen.

1

The Altar Table

The Altar Table is placed in the centre of the Sanctuary against the eastern wall in Christ Church, and is where Holy Communion is celebrated. The height should be between 90 and 102 centimetres and deep and long enough to allow the celebrant to officiate. The top of the Table is called the MENSA and often it has 5 crosses etched in it, one on each corner and one in the centre. These crosses symbolize the 5 wounds in the body of Christ. The Altar Table, whether stone or wood, should be of the finest workmanship the parish can provide. As always, for temporary spaces and emergencies, a simple table will suffice.

Preparing the Altar Table for Holy Eucharist:

Do your service, reverently and when the Nave is empty. Complete your service at least 30 minutes before the worship service begins . Make sure Sanctuary is clean . Place the

Fair Linen on the Altar Table. Pay attention to the liturgical colour of the Altar Frontal, lectern and pulpit hangings when we have them available. Change them if they are not the proper colour for the service. Refer to the Lectionary and/or the "Seasons and Liturgical Colours" section on page 29 of this manual.

A. Vesting the Chalice:

Depending on the presiding Rector's preference, the chalice and paten need to be placed on the Altar Table in a reverent manner. It should be noted that in some Anglican parishes this is placed on the Credence Table and moved to the Altar Table at the time of the offerings.

Step 1

Open the folded **Corporal** and centre it on the Altar at the edge of the Fair Linen, with the embroidered cross toward the priest and upside-down. Place the **Chalice** in the **centre** of the **Corporal**.

Step 2

Place the middle third of a folded **Purificator** over the Chalice, with the end thirds hanging over each side of the Chalice.

Step 3

Place the Paten over the Purificator.

Step 4

Place the Priest's Host (large wafer) in the Paten.

Step 5

Place the **Pall** over the Host and Paten.

Step 6

Place the Veil over the Pall, so that the front edges touch the Altar Table with the cross facing the Nave if there is a cross on the Veil or if there is no cross on the Veil place the Veil over the Pall, so that the front and back edges touch the Altar Table then if the Chalice is empty fold the back of the veil up so that the edge lays over the middle of the pall.

Step 7

Place the Burse on top of the Veiled Chalice if there is no cross on the burse, with opening facing the Nave or standing to the left of the Veiled Chalice if there is a cross on the burse with the Cross facing the Nave.

B. Other Items on the Altar Table:

i. Two Eucharistic or Altar Candles should be placed on the Altar Table, one on either end. However in Christ Church we place six candles on the Retable behind the Altar Table.

ii. The Missal Book on the Missal Stand should also be placed on the Altar Table to the right (your left side) of the dressed chalice.

C. Preparing the Credence Table:

Cover the Credence Table with a Credence Cloth. Place two Cruets at the east (back) side of the Credence Table, with water in them on the left hand side and the Flagon with wine in it on the right hand side. Place the Ciborium or Bread Box, filled with appropriate number of wafers at the right front. Place the Lavabo Bowl at the left front. The Lavabo Towel is placed across the bowl itself or on the Credence Table next to the Lavabo Bowl. Place the Alms Basin (collection plate) or Alms Bag (collection bag) on a shelf underneath the Credence Table; alternatively, place it on a small table nearby the Altar Table but never on the Altar Table. A Flagon filled with extra wine may also be placed on the Credence Table, as needed.

Ambry

An Ambry is the correct name for the box that is locally referred to as the Tabernacle. Reserved elements (blessed wine and bread) may be placed in an Ambry in order to take Holy Communion to those in the hospital or those unable to attend church for other physical or mental illness.

Objects on the Credence Table

D. Preparing for Special Services:

1. Baptism:

   Font: Placed near the entrance to the Nave in an area called the Baptistery, symbolising entrance into the Body of Christ (the Church).

i. Remove the top of the font and set it aside or in the Sacristy.

ii. Place a small table near the font. Cover the table with credence cloth.

   Shell: the silver scallop shaped shell, is used to pour water on the candidate's head.

i. Place the shell on the edge of the font.

   Towel: the baptismal towel should be placed over the edge of the font near the shell or on the small table if necessary.

   Ewer: this water pitcher is made of copper and should be filled less than ½ full with warm water.

Paschal Candle: the Paschal Candle should be lighted and placed nearby.

The priest may ask that the Baptism Certificate and that Anglican Prayer Book marked at Holy Baptism are placed nearby.

The liturgical colour is white.

Items used at Baptism's

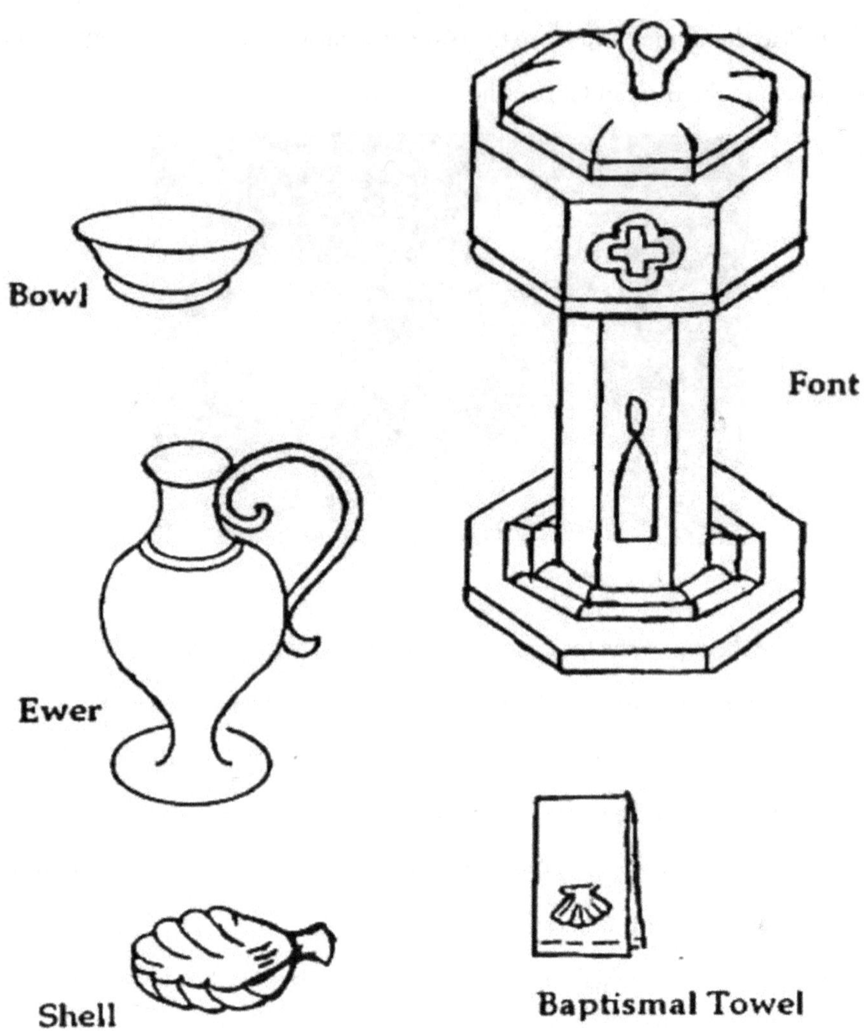

2. Wedding

Altar Guild members should place white flowers in their customary location, usually on the **Retable**. The wedding kneeler should be placed before the **Altar Rale**. If there is no Eucharist, use Altar Candles. The priest decides if decorations may be used in the sanctuary and/or in the nave and Altar Guild members will arrange them. If there is to be a communion, set up the Altar Table as usual for a communion service; however leave room on the Table for the blessing of the rings. Traditionally, there are usually no weddings scheduled during **Advent** or **Lent**, but this is left to the discretion of the priest. The linens and hangings are white.

3. Funeral

Funerals are very sensitive times for families so special care should be taken to follow the guidance of the priest. Flowers may be placed in the church's vases and placed on the Retable and other chosen locations.

i. The **Paschal candle** will be lit by an Acolyte as soon as a body or ashes enter the church and extinguished as soon as it leaves.

ii. It is customary that the funeral **pall** be used on all caskets **for services in the church**. The funeral pall is placed on the back pew by altar guild members. A funeral Pall is always white and covers the coffin.

iii. The Guild of Servers shall meet the coffin at the front doors of the church and **place the pall over the coffin** making sure the pall is cantered and even on all sides.

iv. In the case of an internment of ashes the cremains repository is covered with a cremations pall and place near the **chancel steps**. The priest will place and remove the ashes from the repository.

v. The bell, will "toll" for five minutes after the service rung by the Bell-Ringer. The colour for a funeral and an interment of ashes is **Purple in our Diocese**.

4. After any special service :
   i. The liturgical hangings are all changed back to the colour of the season.
   ii. The sanctuary and nave are readied for the next service.
   iii. The flowers, unless they are to be used for the next service, are taken to the sick, home bound or the bereaved, in the case of funerals.
   iv. The communion vessels, linens, wedding kneeler, special candles, funeral pall, etc. are removed to the sacristy for appropriate care and storage.

E. After the Services:

Wait until the Sanctuary, Chancel, and Nave are empty of congregants before removing the Vessels and Altar Linens to the Sacristy for cleansing. In His service, this should be done quietly and reverently.

1. The Liturgical Rinse
   i. The Chalice, Paten, the corporal and the purificators that came into contact with the consecrated elements should be rinsed and then this "rinse water" should go directly into the piscina at the vestry door.
   ii. These items are treated reverently because they contain "blessed" or "consecrated" bread and wine.

2. The Piscina

The piscine is the sink in the vestry with a drain that goes into the ground rather than into the sewer system.

   i. All consecrated elements to be discarded should be poured into the piscina including wine in chalices, wine rinsed from purificators, wafer that is blessed, crumbs from the paten and ciborium, holy water, sacred oils, blessed ashes.

ii. Baptismal water from the font if the font is emptied should be poured directly into the ground outside the Galilee.

iii. Wash the vessels and the altar linens directly into the piscina.

iv. If you prefer to wash the linins at home then it is perfectly acceptable to take them home, perform the liturgical rinse into a special basin and pour the water into the earth outside the home before beginning the laundering process.

F. Cleansing AFTER the Liturgical Rinse:

1. Chalice

i. The cup of the chalice should be washed in extremely hot soapy water and rinsed in clean extremely hot water, paying special attention to cleaning the rim or lip of the chalice.

ii. To prevent water from getting into the stem, avoid immersing it under the water.

iii. Dry and buff the chalice with a clean, soft, dry cloth. Store in a soft flannel or tarnish proof bag.

2. Paten, Lavabo, Ciborium or Breadbox, Flagon and other Vessels

i. Wash in hot soapy water, rinse in clean hot water. Dry and buff with a clean, soft, dry cloth.

ii. Polish only as necessary.

iii. Use a good quality silver polish, and then wash in hot soapy water, dry, and buff. The silver vessels should be polished only 2 or 3 times a year, using a good silver polish. Do not over polish. In between polishing episodes, wash in hot soapy water, dry, and buff with a soft rag to shine and remove fingerprints

3. Glass Cruets and Flagons

i. Pour remaining water from the water cruet down the piscina.
ii. If there is any consecrated wine in the wine cruet, place it in the Aumbry (Tabernacle) for use later.
iii. Then rinse both cruets with very hot water and drain.
iv. If is a calcite residue on the glass of the Cruet or Flagon, add either a little vinegar or denture tablets and shake them around until the glass is clear, and rinse thoroughly several times with clean very hot water.

4. Linens

i. Any stained linen or linen which does not look fresh should be laundered.
ii. After the liturgical rinse, whether washed in the sacristy or in the home of the assigned altar guild member, the stains should be treated and the linens should be put into soak as soon as possible; soak at least 30-60 minutes.
iii. Hand wash in hot water using a mild laundry soap and rinse thoroughly.
iv. Never put these linens in a dryer.
v. Iron, wrong side up, while the linens are very damp.
vi. Never use starch.
vii. Avoid tugging on or stretching the fabric while ironing it.
viii. Folding should begin after the linens are mostly dry and the ironing has been completed.
ix. The work of caring for the altar linens is to be done solely by altar guild members and under the guidance of the Sacristan.

2

All about the Altar Linens

All worn out altar linens should be burned and the ashes poured into the picina or buried in the earth.

i. Altar linens should be made from good quality linen. Nowadays such linen is fairly easy to maintain.

ii. All of the altar linens have a cross or other liturgical symbols embroidered on them.

iii. These linens may be made by seamstresses.

iv. When making altar linen, always wash and iron the linen first, to avoid shrinkage, before measuring and cutting it.

v. Fine pure cotton thread should be used for all hems and flat embroidery. The embroidery on all linens should be as flat as possible.

vi. When making altar linens, consider acquiring at least one extra set.

vii. In emergency or temporary situations, white napkins and tablecloths made of cloth or even paper may be used.

viii. Suggested Altar linens, necessary for a church with 1 weekly service, are listed below.

2 corporals, 45.72 45.72 cm or 53.34 x 53.34 cm

6 purificators, 30.48 x 30.48 cm

2 palls, 20.32 x 20.32 cm or 17.78 x 17.78 cm

2 lavabo towels, 30.48 x 45.72 cm

1 chalice veil and burse for each season

1 baptismal towel, 30.48 x 45.72 cm

2 fair linen cloths the width of the Altar top, and the length hangs over each end 30.48 cm x 60.96 cm

2 credence cloths, big enough to cover the credence table with a little 'hanging over' all sides

G. The Fair Linen:

i. The Fair Linen is the exact width of the Altar Table, and the length should hang at least 30.48 cm to 60.96 cm over each end.

ii. The cloth should have 5 crosses embroidered on it, one near each corner of the Table, and one in the centre of the Table; if making the fair linen, the hem should be about 5 cm and the corners mitred.

iii. The corner crosses, about 5 cm in diameter.

iv. The Fair Linen Cloth represents Christ's burial shroud.

v. The Fair Linen is never folded.

vi. It is stored on a roller.

H. The Corporal:

i. The Corporal is a linen square with a small cross embroidered on the centre front.

ii. It is the cloth upon which the Chalice is placed.

iii. The corporal is either placed on the centre of the Altar before the service or, if a burse is used, it may be put in the burse to be placed on the altar by the priest.

iv. If making this linen, the hem should be very narrow and the corners mitred and the small cross should be embroidered on the front centre.

v. The Corporal also represents our Lord's face shroud.

vi. The corporal is folded good side up, three folds lengthwise and three folds crosswise.

vii. Folded in this manner, the embroidered cross will not be visible until the Corporal is opened on the Altar.

Corporal Folding Diagram:

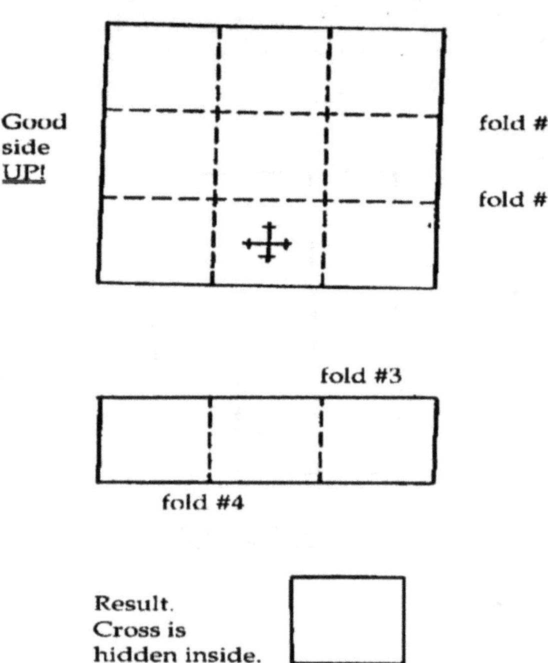

I. The Lavabo Towel

The Lavabo towel is the towel for the Priest's Lavabo.

i. It should be 30.48 x 45.72 cm and made with a narrow (3cm) hem on all sides.

ii. It is embroidered with a small cross or fleur delis lengthwise on the front centre.

iii. The Baptismal towel is the same size as the Lavabo towel, but may have a scallop shaped shell embroidered on it.

iv. Both towels are folded alike as seen on the next page.

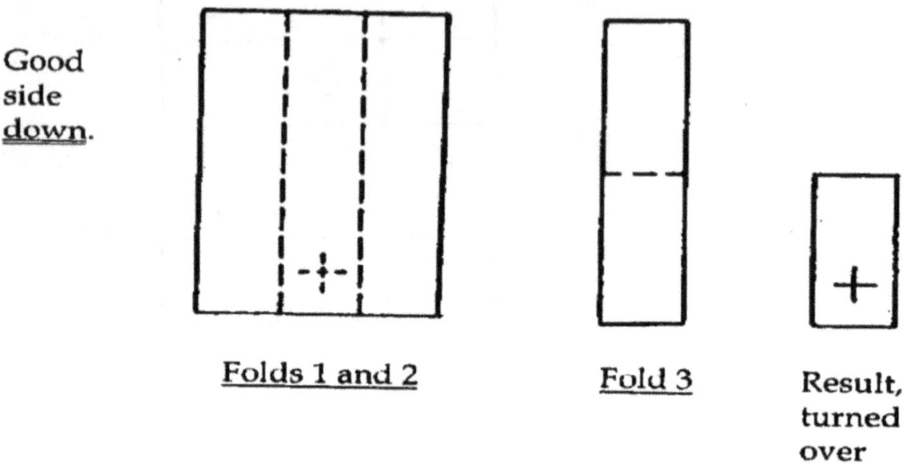

J. The Purificator:

i. The Purificator is 30.48 cm square of linen which is used to wipe the lip of the chalice during the Eucharist.

ii. If making a Purificator, its width and length should be 3 times the diameter of the chalice and the hem should be 1 cm narrow; a white or red 5 cm cross should be embroidered in the exact centre of this linen.

iii. The Purificator is folded in thirds and the cross in the centre third is draped across the chalice during its vesting.

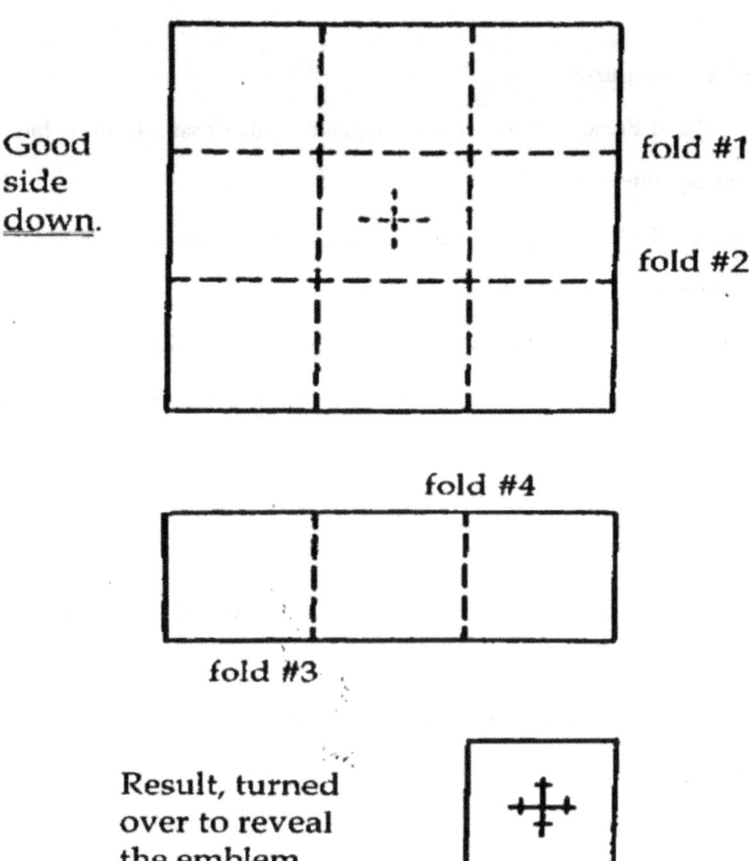

K. The Chalice Pall:

i. The Chalice Pall, which covers the paten, is a white linen square "envelope" into which a hard cardboard or wooden square is placed.

ii. The open end of the linen has a flap to whipstitch or tuck in.

iii. The pall should be large enough to completely cover the paten. Usually 20.32 cm square is sufficient.

iv. The pall may be embroidered with a cross or other symbol which is cantered on one side.

v. The entire pall and lining may be washed and, if dried in the sun, the linen pall will tighten and dry smoothly around the hard square.

vi. If cardboard is used it must be removed for laundering.

L. The Chalice Veil and Burse:

i. The Chalice Veil and Burse, if used, are usually made of silk or satin in the colour of the season and may be quite elaborate.

ii. The chalice veil is a 60.96 cm square which is placed over the vested chalice; it must be large enough to touch the altar on all sides.

iii. The burse is a hinged case, made of two 22.86 cm squares of silk with stiff and hard inserts; it is placed on top or next to the chalice veil and may contain the corporal and the purificators.

M. The Credence Cover:

i. The Credence Cover or Cloth is a white cloth which covers the Credence table and hangs over the top a few inches.

ii. It may be plain or embroidered with a small cross in the centre front.

iii. It may be trimmed in lace.

N. The Under linen:

i. The Under linen, a plain linen cloth, placed directly on top of the altar and is the exact size of the altar top.

ii. The fair linen goes on top of the under linen.

O. The Frontal:

i. The Frontal is the ornamental silk or satin cloth covering the front of the Altar and hanging to the floor.

ii. It may be attached to the protector.

iii. Its colour should be changed with the liturgical season.

P. The Super frontal:

i. The Super frontal is a short silk or satin ornamental cloth covering the front of the altar, hanging about 20 cm from the top of the altar.
ii. It may be used over the frontal or by itself.
iii. Its colour should be changed with the liturgical season.

Q. The Protector:

i. The Protector is a good quality cloth to cover the fair linen between services to protect it.
ii. It usually fits the top of the altar and may be a seasonal, natural, or white colour.
iii. A cross or crosses may be embroidered on the protector.

R. The Pulpit:

i. The Pulpit Fall is a hanging in seasonal colour which is hung, usually by hooks, from the front of the pulpit.

S. The Funeral Pall:

i. The Funeral Pall is a vestment for a casket.
ii. All caskets in a parish are vested with the same pall or with a South African flag for a member of the armed forces.
iii. The pall should be made large enough to cover the casket entirely.
iv. Palls are white, symbolic of the resurrection, and can be simple or ornate, often with one large cross covering the pall.
v. To vest a container of ashes, the white chalice veil may be used.

3

All about the Sacred Vessels

When selecting Eucharistic vessels, precious metals such as silver and gold have been the standard historically. Simple sterling silver is always appropriate, lovely and will last forever if cared for properly. Many churches receive Elements of sacred vessels, often from parishioners in memory of or in honour of loved ones, priests or bishops, etc.

Alternatively, silver plate, glass, or pottery vessels are also appropriate for use at the Lord's Table. Don't use a brass Altar vessel because brass becomes tarnished very quickly with wine and gives a bad taste due to the chemical reaction between the brass and the wine.

One thing to remember when working with the sacred vessels is that metal should never touch metal and the chalice never touches metal or wood. Always use altar linen in between and underneath. For example, a Purificator is always placed over the Chalice BEFORE the paten is placed on the chalice.

For new missions with few resources, for churches recovering from natural disasters, or for churches forced to re-establish their communion vessels "from scratch," a silver plate, clear glass, or pottery goblet may become a chalice. A silver plate, clear glass, or pottery bread and butter plate or salad plate may be used as a paten.

The lavabo, flagon, breadbox or ciborium may be of silver or gold, but also may be of silver plate, clear glass or pottery. In emergency situations, a small clear glass bowl with a secure lid can serve as a breadbox.

The lavabo is a bowl to catch the water used for ceremonial washing of the Priests fingers. The flagon is a pitcher for wine and is larger than the cruet. The breadbox and ciborium contain the wafers or bread for Holy Communion.

The pair of cruets may be either crystal or clear glass. One cruets contain water and wine. Often each cruet has a stopper with a cross on top of it. Glass salad dressing cruets may be substituted as economical alternatives.

4

Clergy Vestments

Priests Vestments - Morning and Evening Prayer

Stole

Cincture

Surplice

Tippet or Preaching Scarf

Cassock

Priests Vestments - For Eucharist Sevices

Cotta worn by Servers

Amice

Alb

Stole

Girdle

Chasuble

Cope

Priest's Vestments:

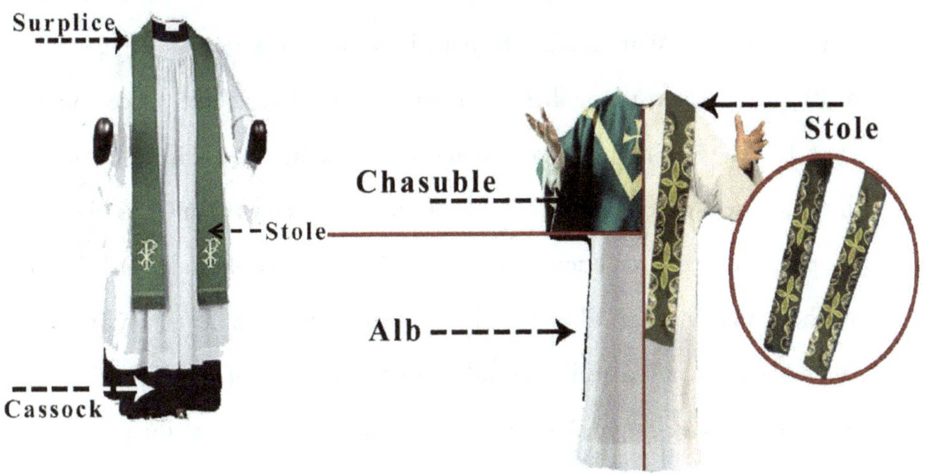

Bishops Vestments:

Bishop Stephen of Matlosane Province

5

Candles

Candles on the Altar may be either Eucharistic candles which are lit for the Eucharist solely, or they may be Altar candles which are lit during any service.

i. Two Altar or Eucharistic candles are usually on the Altar Table, placed on opposite sides of the vested chalice. However Altar candles also may be tall free standing candles, such as pavement candles, on either side of the altar as they are in Christ Church.

ii. There is a great deal of variation in the style and appearance of candles and their holders throughout the Anglican Churches. The holders may be made of any material. The styles and sizes of candles really depend on preference in your worship space.

iii. Most altar guilds are responsible for the care and maintenance of the candles, making certain that they are ready for the next service.

iv. To avoid smoking or flame flaring candles, bees wax candles and their wicks must be trimmed frequently. Pure bees wax candles are the slowest burning and longest lasting.

v. Liquid wax candles look like bees wax candles but each brand is different, so read the care and maintenance instructions carefully.

vi. Tapered candles are not used in the church.

Other types of church candles include:

Candelabra and multiple branched candleholders may be used for special occasions if preferred.

i. Paschal candle: A large pure white candle, on a tall candlestick in the sanctuary; it symbolizes the risen Christ and is lit at services from the Easter Vigil until Pentecost. It is placed at the foot of the chancel steps (or as closely as possible) and lit for baptisms and for funerals when a body or ashes are present.

ii. **Advent wreath:** Four candles, 3 purple and 1 rose, in a circle of greenery, one is lit on each Sunday of **Advent**; the **centre white candle**, known as the **Christ candle**, is lit on Christmas Eve. The five candles are lit until Epiphany. The greenery is often rosemary, holly, fir, mistletoe, cypress, laurel and ivy.

iii. Sanctuary light: A candle within a red glass container, which burns near the Aumbry/tabernacle when it contains consecrated bread and wine. The candle may be electric or battery operated.

6

Flowers

Simplicity is the key word for the use of flowers in the Anglican Church. Flowers and greenery are always fresh or dried. Usually two tasteful arrangements, with the liturgical season and colour in mind, are sufficient in the Sanctuary.

Flower arrangements for the services generally are placed on Retable behind the altar and not on the altar itself. The flowers should enhance the beauty of the sanctuary while blending into the background.

i. The arrangements should never be taller than or compete with the cross, and their design should be classic, Holy Eucharisted, and big enough to be seen, but not too big.

ii. Altar guild or flower guild members should handle and arrange the flowers in vases themselves. Florists or others should never be allowed in the sacristy or in the sanctuary.

iii. Flowers and greenery should never be allowed to wilt and wither in the sanctuary. Before that happens, the flowers may be taken to the ill, the hospitalized, or the home bound. These flowers are given to the Glory of God and are not for personal use.

Weddings:

i. Flowers arranged by the altar guild may be placed in their usual spots. Customs about allowing flowers on the pews vary from church to church, but florists must never enter the sanctuary.

ii. Sanctuary flowers never go to the reception .

Funerals:

Flowers at funerals are not always used. However if flowers are requested or arrive at the church the alter guild members should arrange them in the church's vases and place them in the customary locations.

After the funeral, the flowers go to the home of the bereaved family , or where the family desires.

7

Seasons and Liturgical Colours

The Church Calendar:

Advent, Christmas Epiphany Ash Wednesday Lent Holy week(Palm Sunday, Maundy Thursday, Good Friday, Holy Saturday) Easter Pentecost Trinity Sunday After Pentecost All Saints' Day

i. Purple:

Purple is the colour of and Advent and Lent. It symbolises penitence, sorrow, and also royalty.

Advent, the four Sundays before Christmas Day and the Sunday on or nearest St. Andrew's Day, 30 November. Candles and greens are appropriate during this season.

The Advent wreath has 3 purple candles, one rose (Mary) candle, and a large white candle in the centre, the Christ candle. A candle is lit on the first Sunday; on each following Sunday, an additional candle is lit. The rose candle is lit on the third Sunday. The Christ candle is lit on Christmas Eve. The Advent wreath is covered with greens signifying the Holy Spirit: ivy, laurel, cypress, rosemary, holly, fir, and mistletoe.

Lent, includes 40 days, excluding Sundays which are often called little Easters. Lent extends from Ash Wednesday to Easter Eve.

Purple is used from Ash Wednesday until Palm Sunday and the cross is veiled in sheer purple.

ii. White:

White is the colour of Christmas, Epiphany, The Baptism of our Lord, All Saints' Day, Easter, Transfiguration Day, Ascension Day, and Trinity Sunday.

It symbolises purity and new birth.

White is used for weddings, baptisms, funerals and other special occasions.

Christmas season begins on Christmas Eve and continues through the twelve days of Christmas until Epiphany, on January 6

Epiphany celebrates the arrival of the Magi on the 6th and it ends on Shrove Tuesday. The colour changes from White to Green after the first Sunday of Epiphany.

Easter begins with the Easter Vigil.

The Paschal candle is placed in the sanctuary through Pentecost Sunday.

iii. Green

Green is the colour of ordinary time, from Pentecost until Advent.

Green symbolises spring, life and growth in the Holy Spirit.

iv. Red

Holy Week includes Palm Sunday, Maundy Thursday, Good Friday, and Holy Saturday. On Palm Sunday the colour is changed to Red and remains Red through the Maundy Thursday service.

Red is used for Holy Week and Pentecost (Whitsunday), Confirmation, Ordination, and Feast Days.

Red is indicative of the Holy Spirit and Martyrdom, the days of the martyred saints are red.

v. Black

On Good Friday the cross is veiled in sheer black and the altar is bare.

8

Symbols of Christianity

SYMBOL SIGNIFICANCE	SYMBOL SIGNIFICANCE	SYMBOL
ALPHA-OMEGA	eternally of Christ	
ANCHOR	faith	
BREAD AND WINE	Eucharist--death of Christ	
CHI-RHO	first two letters of "Christ" in Greek	
CROSS	death of Christ (Celtic Cross symbol of unity between Heaven and Earth	
DOVE	Holy Spirit at baptism of Christ	

FIRE	Holy Spirit on Day of Pentecost	
FISH	initial letters of "Jesus Christ, God's son, Saviour" in Greek, spelling ICHTHUS, the Greek word for "fish"; feeding of 5000; "fishers of men"	 ΙΧΘΥΣ
LAMB	Christ's self-sacrifice	
SHEPHERD	Christ's care for His people	
SHIP	Church (Noah's ark; cf. baptism)	
VINE	Christ's union with His people; wine of eucharis	

9

Liturgical space inside the Church of Christ Church

The two sides of a Church:

1. **Gospel Side:** on the side that the pulpit is on when facing the altar it is on your left hand side. Deacons, other Priests, lay ministers, church wardens, sacristans and servers may sit in the Sedilia on the Gospel side of the Apse.
2. **Epistle Side:** the lectern is on the Epistle Side when facing the altar it is on your right hand side. The choir sit in the Choir-stalls on the Epistle Side.

The Layout of the Church:

1. **Galilee:** An entry porch of a Gothic style church like Christ Church in Beaufort West.
2. **Baptistery:** An area at the back of the Nave where baptisms take place. It contains the font and ewer at all time. Traditionally unbaptised people may not enter the Nave of the Church and for this reason there are also pews for the unbaptised to sit in in the Baptistery. Furthermore, women with new born babies that are unbaptised sit here, it is also a place where people who are excommunicated from the Church or who are under ecclesiastic interdict (a form of Church discipline where someone is suspended from taking Holy Eucharist) sits. This is also the reason for the Font being at the back of the Church, so that people are baptised in the Baptistery that is separate from the Nave.
3. **Nave:** The area of the church containing the pews where the Baptised parishioners sit.

4. **Apse:** This is the liturgical space containing the Choir-stalls, Sedilia and the Officiant's desks.
5. **Sanctuary:** is that part of the church beyond the altar rail. No person besides Clergy, lay clergy, servers and sacristans may enter the Sanctuary at any time of day or night. The only exception being when a person who is in fear of their life may enter the Sanctuary and clutch or hold onto the Altar, people may only seek sanctuary if they have been baptised and have partaken in Holy Eucharist on the preceding Easter Sunday.

The Furniture of the Church:

1. **High Altar:** The High Altar (main altar) is the table where the Eucharistic celebration takes place. It is located in the east end of the church; the liturgy (worship) is supposed to be celebrated with the priest and the congregants facing east known as **Ad Orientem** because it is the direction whence Jesus will come again.
2. **Pew:** is a long bench seat used for seating members of a congregation church.
3. **Kneeler:** a piece of furniture used for resting in a kneeling position during Christian prayer. It may be covered by a cushion called a hassock.
4. **Tuffet:** is a low stool where only a single person may kneel at a time.
5. **Hassock:** is a cushion for kneeling on in church, while at prayer.
6. **Choir-stalls:** where the choir sit on the Gospel side of the Chancel.
7. **Officiants Desk:** is a table connected to a chair where the Vicar, Curate, (a member of the clergy appointed to assist a Vicar), Deacon or a Lay-Minister sits when they officiate during a Church service or ceremony.
8. **Sedilia:** Where Priests, Deacons, lay ministers, church wardens, sacristans and servers sit when they are not officiating during a Church service or ceremony. It is

found on the Epistle Side of the Chancel. It is that area immediately in front of and three steps up above the nave behind the Rood Screen. People who come to confession sit in the Sedilia and confess to the Priest who receives their confession from the Sanctuary. However the priest may come out of the Sanctuary and receive the confession in the Sedilia then return to the Sanctuary to grant absolution to the confessor.

9. **Bishops Throne:** is on the Gospel side of the High Altar. When the Bishop is not in attendance at a Parish Church then the Rector is seated in the Bishops Throne as the Judicial and Spiritual head of the Church.
10. **Vicars Chair:** the Vicar of a Parish will sit in a lesser chair on the Epistle side of the Sanctuary near the Credence Table.
11. **Credence Table:** is on the Epistle side of the Sanctuary. This is where the utensils, Water, Wine and Bread used for the Holy Eucharist are located.
12. **Votive Rack:** is a stand in a Church where people come to make a votive offering. They put a coin in the Votive Box, light a small candle, typically made of beeswax to be burnt as a votive offering while they pray in the Church. They do not pray at the Votive Rack but go and sit in a pew where they meditate and pray.
13. **Situla:** Is a container at the Galilee that holds Holy Water. When people enter a Church they should use holy water and making a sign of the cross that reflects the renewal of their baptism, this is a cleansing from venial sin (a venial sin is a lesser sin that does not result in a complete separation from God), as well as providing protection against evil. The following prayer is said, "*By this Holy water and by your Precious Blood, wash away all my sins O Lord*".

Other Rooms of the Church:

1. **Sacristy:** The room(s) usually behind or near the sanctuary where the sacred vessels are stored, prepared and cleansed.

2. **Vestry:** This is where vestments and other supplies are stored, prepared, and where Clergy, laity and servers dress before a service. It is also the non-observed liturgical space where members of the altar guild do their work and where the priests and servers gather to prepare for services.

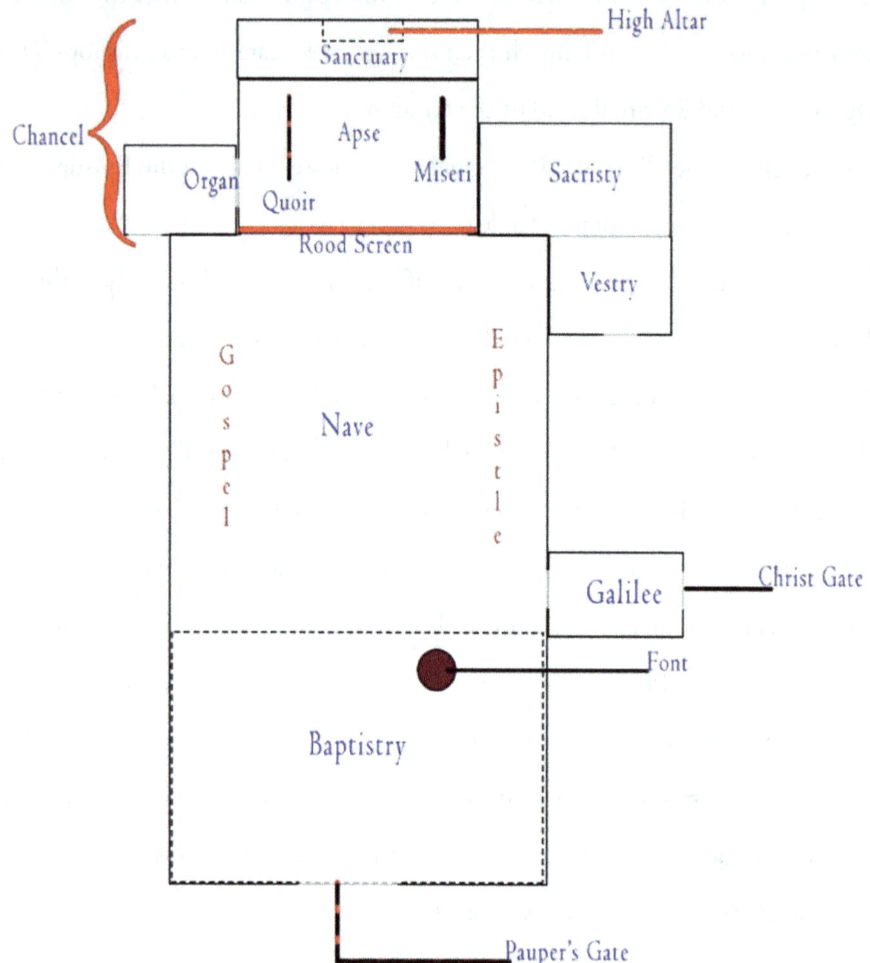

10

Setting up the Sacristy and the Vestry

The sacristy and the Vestry is the room on the south side of the church where the clergy, lay ministers and servers are able to vest and where the altar guild does its work.

The Vestry should contain cupboards for vestments and should also contain a vesting table or chest of drawers.

Traditionally the priest's vestments are arranged on the vesting table in the order, in which they were worn, with the chasuble or Cope on the bottom. However at Christ Church, vestments seem to fare better on hangers in the cupboards.

The Sacristy and the Vestry contain:

1. A piscina, which includes a tap for rinsing the consecrated elements directly into the piscine. It is a regular sink with hot and cold water.
2. Cabinets for altar vestments, the liturgical hangings, frontals, super-frontals
3. Cupboards for cleaning supplies, i.e. laundry soaps, silver polish Cabinets for flower arranging supplies and vases
4. A cupboard for the clergy's vestments
5. A cupboard for lay ministers and servers vestments
6. A secure safe or locking cupboard for the sacred vessels; the unopened communion wine may be stored on the floor of this vestry
7. A countertop work space.
8. A desk containing organizational information: an inventory of all the altar vesting and linens and sacred vessels, a checkout and return list of linens being prepared by a member away from the church, an order list for supplies, a flower chart, and the altar guild instructions for each service.

11

Thurifer

"The use of incense is an ancient custom in liturgical prayer. It signifies the prayer and offering of the Church during the Sacred Liturgy rising to the sight of God. Incense is customarily used during celebrations of the Sacred Liturgy on Sundays and solemnities, especially at the Eucharist Service." –

Outline of Incense during Holy Eucharist

Incense is used in the following manner:

1. during the Entrance Procession (Thurifer leads procession);
2. at the beginning of Holy Eucharist to incense the Cross and altar;
3. at the procession before the Gospel and the proclamation of the Gospel;
4. after the bread and chalice have been placed on the altar, to incense the offerings, the cross, and the altar, as well as the Priest and the people;
5. at the elevation of the host and chalice during the Consecration of the Eucharistic Prayer;
6. And in the Recessional. Incense is also used during the Easter Season and Funeral Liturgies:
   i. for the incensation of the Paschal Candle
   ii. For the reverence of the remains of the deceased during Funeral Liturgies as a sign of the dignity of the human body and of the Resurrection of Christ.

The Use of Incense:

Three Swings

The following are incensed with 3 swings of the Thurible:

1. the Blessed Sacrament; a relic of the Holy Cross or image of the Lord; the offerings of bread and wine during the Preparation of the Elements; the Altar Cross; the
2. Book of the Gospels; the Paschal Candle; priest celebrants; and the assembly."

Two Swings

The following are incensed with 2 swings of the Thurible:

1. at the beginning of the Sacred Liturgy during the incensation of the altar
2. Relics and images of Saints."

One Swing

The altar is to be incensed with single swings of the Thurible:

12

Thurifer Procedures

Before Holy Eucharist

1. Sign In at the Vestry 30 minutes before Holy Eucharist and Vest.
2. Place stand for Thurible at Baptismal font. (Boat Server will assist in putting stand out and making sure incense boat is full)
3. Light 2 charcoal 15 minutes before Holy Eucharist outside in an open area
4. Be careful of sparks to clothing/vestment/yourself and never place Thurible on wooden Tables or credence tables. Place lighted charcoal (hollow side up) in Thurible
5. Before Holy Eucharist, stand with Thurible and boat the open in the Apse under high-ceiling rood loft.

Procession and Beginning of Holy Eucharist

1. Ask the Priest or Priest to add 2 scoops of incense before procession begins.
2. Lead procession swinging Thurible and the boat server walks next to you carrying boat
3. Hold Thurible with thumb in ring, hand in a fist. Swing smoking Thurible forward and backward by moving your wrist slightly (not your arm). Pace procession slowly, reverently leading assembly into prayer, filling the space with sweet fragrance.
4. When arriving at steps, stand at Gospel side, facing Altar
5. Take care not to hit candles/plants while swinging Thurible. Bow head when the Priest bows
6. Walk up steps toward the Altar

7. The Boat Server first gives the Priest the boat, and then hold Thurible while Priest puts incense in, then exchange the Thurible with Priest. Be careful, Thurible will be hot!
8. Give your attention to the objects that the Priest incenses
9. Receive Thurible back from Priest
10. Walk down steps; place Thurible and boat on stand near you
11. Sit where designated in the Sedilia or with Altar Servers.

Gospel Acclamation and Incensing of Book of Gospels

1. At start of Gospel Acclamation, remove Thurible and boat from stand and stand behind Baptism font.
2. If the Bishop is present, wait until the Deacon has been blessed by the Bishop, take Thurible and boat to the Bishops chair. Hold Thurible for the Bishop to put incense in.
3. When there is a Priest then go to the priest with the Boat Server so that he can put incense into Thurible and bless it.
4. Process in front of the Gospel procession to halfway down the aisle.
5. Give the Thurible to the Deacon to incense the Bible. Receive Thurible back from Deacon.
6. Step back to a location behind and to the right of Deacon.
7. Gently swing Thurible throughout Gospel reading. Ensure you do not block line of sight to Priest's chair.
8. Give your attention to the proclamation of Gospel
9. After "Praise to Christ our Lord" turn, take five paces towards the Chancel, stop and wait for the rest of the gospel party to get into procession behind, then move forward in procession to the altar.

10. During the peace, add 1 charcoal to the Thurible after lighting it

Blessing of the Offering

1. When the Deacon holds the collection to the Priest and go give the Priest the Thurible to incense the offering.

The Eucharist

After the table is prepared:

1. Hold the Thurible for Priest to put incense in.
2. Exchange Thurible with Priest and then go back down one step and wait for Priest to incense the Cross.
3. Give your attention to the Elements and Altar while they are being incensed.
4. Receive Thurible back from Priest. The Priest will bow, Thurifer will bow and incense Priest with three swings of the Thurible.
5. Turn and go in front of altar at the top of the steps. Bow to the congregation, swing the Thurible two times to the front, turn and swing Thurible 2x to the left side, and turn and swing Thurible 2x to the right side of the church. Bow again facing the front.
6. Return Thurible and boat to stand and return to your seat.

Consecration

1. Move to the front of the altar on the ground level of the Apse during the Holy, Holy, Holy Lord. (2 scoops of incense are placed on the coals in the Thurible during the Epiclesis). Note: The epiclesis, in which, by means of particular invocations, the Church implores the power of the Holy Spirit that the Elements offered by human hands be consecrated.
2. When the Priest lifts up the Blessed Sacrament, incense it (3 swings, 3 times).

Recession

Before the Priest leaves the Chair (after the final blessing):

1. Add 2 scoops of incense to Thurible
2. Take Thurible and boat and move to the centre aisle, facing the altar swinging Thurible using your whole arm.
3. Slight bow of head when Priest bows
4. Lead recession at a faster pace than was done for the procession, (normal walking pace) leading assembly into their mission for Christ in the world.

After Holy Eucharist

1. Dispose of charcoals and incense in Thurible in stones on left side outside the Vestry
2. Be certain that charcoals are complete extinguished, if not get a cup of water and extinguish!
3. The Boat Server will help you extinguish and return Thurible and boat to the vestry.

Reminders

1. Anytime you are standing still with the Thurible, gently swing the Thurible to keep air flowing through the Thurible.
2. When swinging the Thurible, keep your elbow close to your side.
3. Use the tongs for picking up and loading the charcoal to avoid getting charcoal on your hands or cloths.
4. Make sure the charcoal is well lit before placing in the Thurible.
5. When incensing the congregation, do not lean into the swings, but keep your feet together and swing only using your wrist.

13

Crucifer and Acolyte Procedure

Check assignments, get questions answered by the Sub Deacon on duty or if needed, Deacon Mark or celebrant.

- Make sure and the elements (bread and wine) are with the offertory bags in at the entrance to the Nave on the vestibule table .
- Acolyte - 5 minutes before the service (e.g. 08:55AM), light candles.
- 1st light the Pascal candle, if present, at left hand side of the Altar as you face it. 2nd light Gospel candles on the right hand side of the Altar Light the Gospel Eucharist Candle First . Last, light the Epistle candles on the left side of the altar.
- Paschal candle is burned from the Easter Vigil until Pentecost, at funerals and baptisms.
- Advent Wreath is only used during Advent season .
- Crucifer goes to the vestry and picks up the processional cross at 08:55 AM.
- Crucifer brings the cross to the Galilee for the formation of the procession. If you are a Server when you are ready for service, wait at the Bell Tower.
- Keep talking to minimum, no playing around; the Galilee is a place where enter the Church, a time when we are to be in a spiritual state. Be reverent, you are setting an example.

Processional:

⌖ We process from the Galilee.

⌖ Line up for procession in this order:

1. Thurifer
2. Crucifer
3. Acolytes
4. Lay Ministers
5. Deacon
6. Priest

- Crucifer hold cross straight and high up (Caution: make sure the cross will miss the Screen). Never bow with Cross in your hands .
- Begin half way thru the 1st verse of the Processional hymn or when the Celebrant or Deacon tells you to begin. Start with left foot and proceed with reverence.
- Process to Altar, STOP in front for a moment and then turn to left, place cross in holder, go to your seat and stand with Congregation to finish the processional hymn.
- Follow the Eucharistic Prayers and Prayers of the People in an Anglican Prayer Book.

  See Bulletin for correct collect.

- ALL Stand for the Holy Gospel. Nicene Creed face the altar, Prayers of the People, Confession, Peace and Eucharistic Prayer.
- Offertory Song is Acolyte's cue to serve the celebrant in preparation of the Table (Altar) for Holy Communion.

Offertory:

- "The peace of the Lord be with you…" cue for Acolytes to assist Deacon and Lay minister in preparation of the Lord's Table for Communion. Each priest will have slight variations in what they want.

  Be flexible, you are here to serve.

  Deacon or Lay minister will need the Corporal, large Ciborium, blessed water and host from the Credence Table.
- Always hand to the Deacon or Lay minister the water cruet with your right hand, handle toward him or her. Receive vessels in your left hand.
- Deacon or Lay minister may call for the bread and wine (elements) before or after preparing the Altar (table).
- Ushers will bring the elements (sacramental bread and wine) forward to the altar and give to the Celebrant from the back of the Nave.
- Stand and be prepared to receive the offering plate and bags if the Celebrant does not wish to put them on the Altar.
- Offering plate and bags should be placed on the Credence table at the back on the left hand side.

Great Thanksgiving Crucifers place:

- Stand with the Celebrant, Deacon and Lay Ministers, for the Eucharistic Prayer, Lord's Prayer, and Fractional.
- Remain standing with Lay Ministers.
- Your spot is to the right of the Gospel side of the altar.

Acolytes:

- Acolytes Kneel on the Epistle Side of the Altar.

Diagram of a High Altar in Ad Orientem

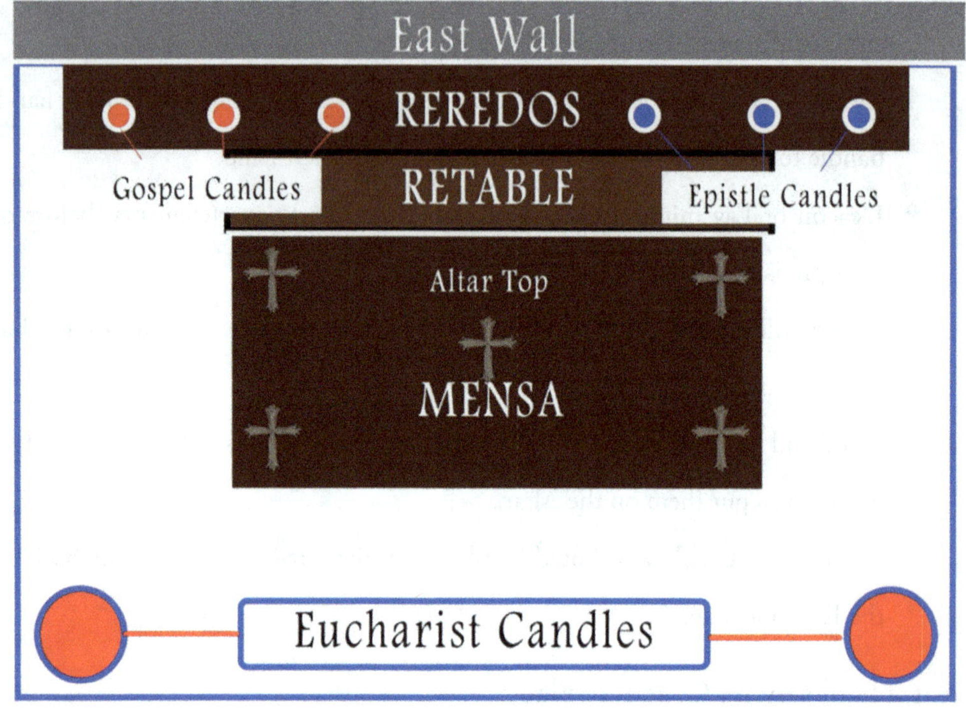

After Communion:

- When communion is over, assist the Deacon or lay minister in clearing the Altar.
- Place the used Purificator(s) in the chalice(s), if chalice is empty. If not, place on top of the chalice before the ciborium, and pall. Place the Host (Bread) basket at the back of the Credence Table between the Gospel and Offering baskets.

Recessional:

- Crucifer move to Cross at the Altar at the beginning of the music.
- Remove the Cross from the stand when singing begins (1st Verse).
- Move to the front of the Altar looking to the back of the Church.
- Begin recessional procession with your left foot at the beginning of the 2nd verse.
- Go out in same order as coming in Thurifer, Crucifer, Acolyte, Lay Ministers, Deacon, Priest
- Crucifer will leave the Procession during the song. Returning the cross to the holder next to the Credence table, by going to the left (Gospel) side of the church and taking the candle snuff returning to the back of the church and re-joining the procession snuffing the Acolytes candles then handing the Snuffer to an acolyte before the second last verse is sung.

After Processional:

- During the last verse of the processional hymn (closing song). Acolyte will extinguish altar candles.
- Move to and face the front of the altar.
- At the end of the hymn reverently extinguish the altar candles in opposite order, Gospel 1st (on Left as you face the Altar); Epistle 2nd (on Right as you face the Altar). Do not cross the Altar without bowing.

- Finally the Pascal candle or Advent wreath if present, before the Dismissal by the Celebrant or Deacon.

After Service:

- Put vestments and cross away neatly.
- Clean out snuffers with tissue.
- If an Alb needs to be cleaned fold it neatly and place on the chair. Any of the equipment is in need of cleaning or repairs, let Lay Deacon or member of the Altar Guild know.

14

Commonly Used Terms

Ablutions: Ceremonial cleansing of the chalice and paten by the celebrant after the Eucharist.

Acolyte: One who assists the priest and carries the candles.

Advent Wreath: Four candles arranged in a circle, one of which is lighted on the first Sunday in Advent, and one more on each of the following Sundays in Advent. A white candle, the Christ Candle, is placed in the centre of the circle and lighted on Christmas Eve, and thereafter during the Christmas season. See page 24.

Alb: The long white robe which the priest wears for services of Holy Eucharist.

Alms Basin: An offering plate.

Altar: The Holy Table upon which the Holy Eucharist is celebrated.

Altar Bread: The wafers or bread used at the Eucharist.

Altar Rail: A railing in front of the altar that separates the chancel from the rest of the church.

Amice: A large oblong white neck piece worn by some priests with the Alb.

Aumbry or Tabernacle: The 'wall cabinet' in the sanctuary that contains consecrated bread and wine.

Baptistery: The place where the font is located, usually near the entrance of the church.

Baptismal Towel: The long, narrow towel which the celebrant uses to 'dry off' the newly baptized. For baptisms we put out one baptismal towel for each person to be baptized.

Bible Markers: The silk hangings which decorate the lectern.

Bishop: The highest order of the sacred ministry in the Anglican Church; the head of the Diocese, elected by the Diocese.

Bishop Coadjutor: A bishop elected and given jurisdiction to assist and later to succeed the diocesan Bishop.

Bishop Suffragan: A bishop elected to assist the diocesan bishop, but without jurisdiction or right of succession.

Bishop's Chair: A special chair on the gospel side of the sanctuary, reserved for the diocesan bishop on his visitations.

Bread Boxes: Small, round or square, silver 'boxes' with lids which hold the wafers for the Eucharist.

Burse: A square flat case used to hold the corporal, the post communion veil, if used, and Purificator. It is placed on the veiled chalice at the Eucharist.

Cassock: The long black garment which the priest wears during his every day duties and under a white surplice for services that are not Eucharist services. On Good Friday black cassocks are worn without the surplice.

Celebration: The consecration and administration of the Holy Eucharist.

Thurible: A vessel for burning incense; especially, a covered incense burner swung on chains in a religious ceremony.

Cere Cloth: The protective cloth which goes on the altar between the frontal and the fair linen. This protects the linen of the frontal and the altar from wine spills.

Chalice: The 'goblet' from which wine is served.

Chalice Veil: See Post-Communion Veil and Silk Chalice Veil.

Chancel: The area which contains the choir pews, the organ, the pulpit, the lectern, and the altar.

Chasuble: The 'poncho-shaped' garment which the celebrant wears for the Eucharist. On Sundays the priest puts it on at the Offertory.

Chimere: A long garment with arm holes, but without sleeves. It is worn by a bishop over the rochet and may be either red or black.

Ciborium: A chalice like cup with a cover, used for the bread at the Eucharist. It may be used in place of the bread box.

Cincture: A wide flat cloth belt or girdle worn around the cassock.

Cope: A long, elaborate cloak of coloured silk or brocade worn by a bishop or priest at festival occasions. It has a clasp at the neck called a Morse.

Cotta: A white garment similar to a surplice, but shorter and without a cross on the front worn by choir and servers over the red cassock.

Credence Table or Shelf: The shelf on the Epistle (pulpit) side of the Altar. This table holds the wine and wafers to be consecrated, the lavabo bowl, and the lavabo towel.

Credence Table Cover or Credence Cloth: The linen cover which is placed on the credence table before the table is 'set'.

Crozier: A bishop's pastoral staff.

Crucifer: The cross-bearer in a procession.

Crucifix: The cross with the figure of our Lord upon it.

Cruets: The small pitchers which hold wine and water. The cruet containing wine is always kept to the right side of the water. When the cruets are placed on the credence table, the handles are toward the wall if there is an acolyte to serve the priest, or toward the nave when the priest is alone.

Deacon: One of three holy orders of the ministry.

Dean: The chief of the clergy on the staff of a cathedral; also the head of a seminary.

Diocese: The see or jurisdiction of a bishop.

Dossal: A tapestry or curtain which hangs behind the altar.

Dust Cover: The linen cloth which covers the altar fair linen after the worship service is over. A dust cover is often of a coarser weave of linen than the fair linen. It is simply a dust cover, even though it may be embroidered with crosses, etc.

Elements: The bread, wine, and water which are used at the Eucharist.

Epistle Side: The right side of the chancel as one faces the altar.

Eucharist: The service of Holy Communion.

Eucharistic Candlesticks: The pair of big wooden candlesticks in Christ Church that stand on either side of the altar at 45° to the front corner of the altar. These candles are lit only and when the Eucharist is celebrated. These are the only candles that go on the altar or in our case stand next to the altar.

Eucharistic Vessels: Any or all of the containers and 'dishes' used for the Eucharist.

Eucharistic Vestment: The special vestments often worn at a celebration of the Eucharist or Holy Communion: Alb, amice, girdle, stole, chasuble, and maniple.

Ewer: The large pitcher which holds water for baptisms. When there is a baptism, the ewer is filled with hot water just before the service, and placed on a small table near the font.

Fair Linen: The large white linen cloth which covers the altar, on top of the cere cloth. It is the altar's tablecloth.

Flagon: A vessel to hold wine for the Eucharist.

Followers: The brass 'collars' which fit the tops of the candles to protect against drafts.

Font: The basin where baptisms are performed.

Frontal: A full-length, coloured hanging for the altar.

Girdle: A white cotton or linen rope worn about the waist over the alb. Black girdles are sometimes worn over the cassock.

Gospel Book: The book which contains all of the Gospel readings.

Gospel side: The left side of the chancel as once faces the altar.

Hangings: All of the coloured silk items that decorate the sanctuary and chancel.

Host Wafer or Priest's Host: The large wafer which is held up and broken by the celebrant at the Eucharist.

Hymn Board: The wooden board on the wall of a church which lists the day of the church season and the hymns for the day.

IHS: The first three letters of the name of Jesus in Greek. Also the initial letters of Iesus hominem salvator, Latin for "Jesus the Saviour of mankind".

Lavabo Bowl: The small silver bowl which is used by the priest for the symbolic washing of hands before celebrating the Eucharist. It is placed on the credence table with the lavabo towel.

Lavabo Towel: The small linen towel on the credence table, next to the lavabo bowl, with which the priest dries his/her hands after the symbolic washing of hands before celebrating the Eucharist.

Lectern: The podium from which the lessons are read.

Lectionary or Text Book: The book which contains all the Sunday Bible readings for the year. Texts change from Year A to Year B to Year C beginning with the first Sunday in Advent.

Liturgical Colours: The appropriate colour for the day according to the church calendar. It is the colour of the hangings and the colour of the priest's vestments. The calendar on the wall of the sacristy has the days printed in the appropriate colour.

The basic seasonal colours are:

Advent--- Purple or Blue

Christmas--- White

Epiphany--- Green

Lent--- Purple

Easter ---White

Pentecost--- Red

Trinity Sunday ---White

Sundays after Pentecost ---Green

Litany Desk: The portable kneeling bench or prayer desk.

Maniple: A short band or scarf worn on the left arm of the celebrant at Holy Communion as part of the Eucharistic Vestments. Most priests no longer use a maniple.

Mensa: The top of the altar or Holy Table.

Book of Common Prayer or Missal: Now known as AN ANGLICAN PRAYER BOOK (APB). The Altar Service Book, containing the services of the Holy Eucharist, the collects, epistles, and gospels.

Missal Stand or Service Book Stand: The stand or desk upon which the Altar Service Book rests.

Mitre: A liturgical headdress worn by bishops on formal occasions.

Oblations: The bread and wine brought to the altar at the offertory.

Oblation Table: A table which holds the bread and wine, the 'oblations', which are to be brought forward by members of the congregation during the offertory.

Offertory: The bringing of oblations and alms to the altar.

Office: A service of the church, other than Holy Eucharist, such as Morning or Evening Prayer.

Office Candles or Office Lights: The candles behind the altar on the retable next to the cross in the sanctuary. These candles, which are lit for all services, are often on three unbranched candle holders on each side of the cross. Some churches use three or seven branched candelabra.

Ordination: The conferring of Holy Orders by a bishop.

Orphrey: An embroidered band on a chasuble or other vestment or hanging.

Pall: This word means 'covering'. It refers to two quite different coverings:

1. A pall is the small, linen covered square of Plexiglas which we use to cover the paten and host wafer on a vested chalice.
2. The funeral pall is the large, embroidered silk covering which covers the casket for a funeral.

Paschal Candle: The large, decorated candle which is lit at the Easter Vigil and burns throughout the Easter season to Pentecost. The Paschal candle is also used at baptisms and funerals.

Paten: The silver plate from which the communion wafers are served.

Pectoral Cross: The large cross worn by ordained priests and bishops.

Piscina: A drain in the sacristy which goes directly to the ground instead of into the sewer system. It is used for the disposal of consecrated elements: wine in chalices, bread crumbs on paten, and wine rinsed from purificators.

Priest: The second of the three orders of the priesthood; one who has been ordained by a bishop to administer the Sacraments of the Church.

Protector: Another word for dust cover.

Pulpit Fall: The decorative silk rectangle which hangs from the pulpit.

Purificator: The small linen square which the priest or other minister uses to wipe the rim of the chalice; acts like a napkin.

Rector: A priest who is head of a parish.

Reserved Sacrament: Consecrated bread and wine, the Body and Blood of Christ, which has not been distributed to communicants in a service of Holy Eucharist, and is kept in an ambry or tabernacle. A small amount of consecrated bread and wine is often reserved for use by the priest and lay ministers in visitations, or for the sick, dying, or other similar circumstances.

Retable: A shelf behind the altar, also called a gradine.

Rochet: A long white linen vestment with wide sleeves tied at the wrists, worn by a bishop under a chimere.

Rood: A cross or crucifix.

Sacristy: A room where preparations are made for the worship service, the Lord's Kitchen. In addition to the Altar Guild sacristy where we work, there is often a priest's sacristy where the priest and acolytes vest.

Sanctuary: The space inside the altar rail.

Sanctuary Light: A light, usually a candle but not necessarily so, in the sanctuary that is constantly lit whenever there is reserve sacrament present in the ambry or tabernacle.

Service Book or Missal: The large 'prayer book' from which the priest reads the service at the altar.

Service Book Stand: See 'Missal Stand'. The stand which holds the service book on the altar.

Silk Chalice Veil: A square covering of silk or brocade used to cover the chalice and paten before and after the Eucharist.

Stole: A long narrow band of silk worn over the shoulders of the clergy at the Eucharist. It is worn over the Alb, and usually matches the colour of the hangings.

Super frontal or Frontlet: A short hanging for the front of the altar it may be used over a frontal or separately, and may be made of handsome lace or silk.

Surplice: A white vestment with full flowing sleeves. It is longer than a cotta and has a cross on the front. Worn with the stole, it is the standard clergy vesture for any of the church's offices.

Thurible: A censer. A vessel for burning incense; especially a covered incense burner swung on chains in a religious ceremony.

Tippet: A black scarf, wider than a stole, worn about the neck, with ends hanging down the front. It is worn by the clergy at choir offices. Usually the diocesan shield and the shield of the priest's seminary are on the ends of the tippet.

Vested Chalice: The chalice, covered by a pacificator, paten and host wafer, ready to be used by the priest. A priest's host is not placed on the paten when the host is being presented from the oblation table.

Vestments: The special garments worn by the priest and other ministers of the service.

Vicar: A priest in charge of a mission or chapel

Wafer: The unleavened bread used at the Eucharist.

Notes:

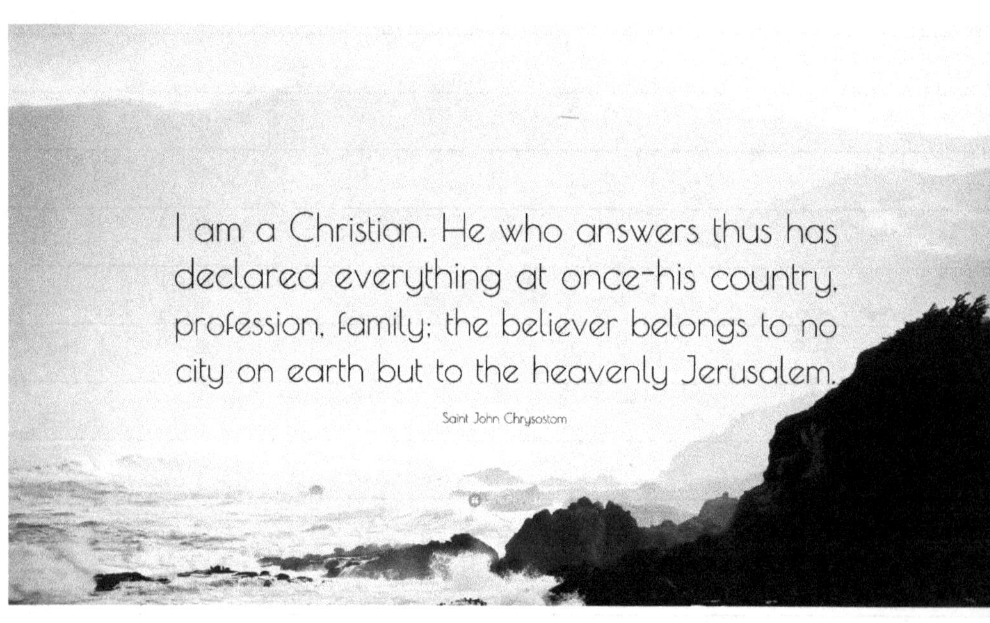
I am a Christian. He who answers thus has declared everything at once-his country, profession, family; the believer belongs to no city on earth but to the heavenly Jerusalem.
Saint John Chrysostom

Whether or not our prayer is heard depends not on the number of our words, but on the fervor of our souls.
Saint John Chrysostom

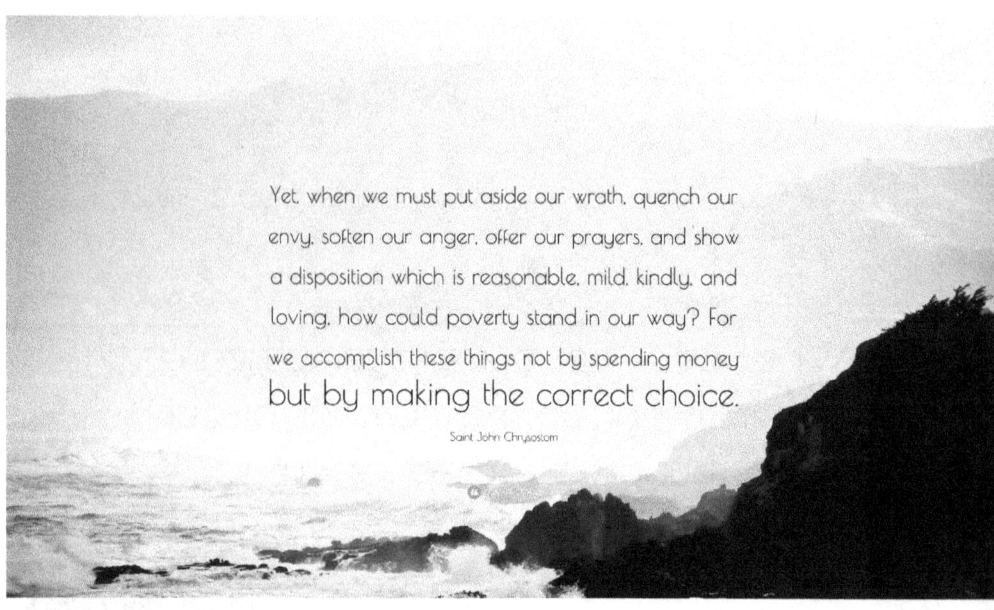
Yet when we must put aside our wrath, quench our envy, soften our anger, offer our prayers, and show a disposition which is reasonable, mild, kindly, and loving, how could poverty stand in our way? For we accomplish these things not by spending money but by making the correct choice.
Saint John Chrysostom

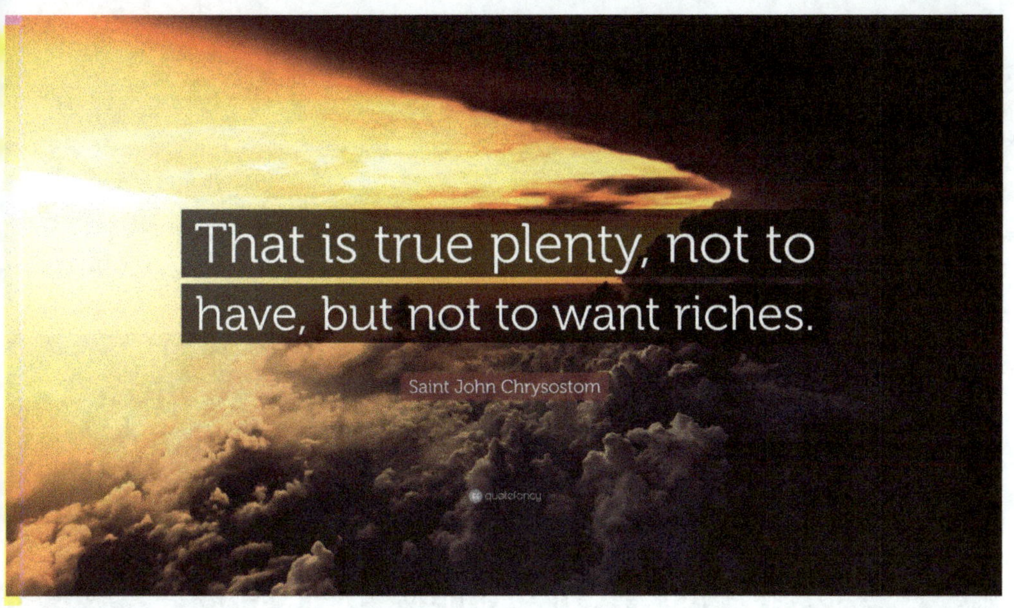
That is true plenty, not to have, but not to want riches.
Saint John Chrysostom
quotefancy

Even if we stand at the very summit of virtue, it is by mercy that we shall be saved.

Saint John Chrysostom

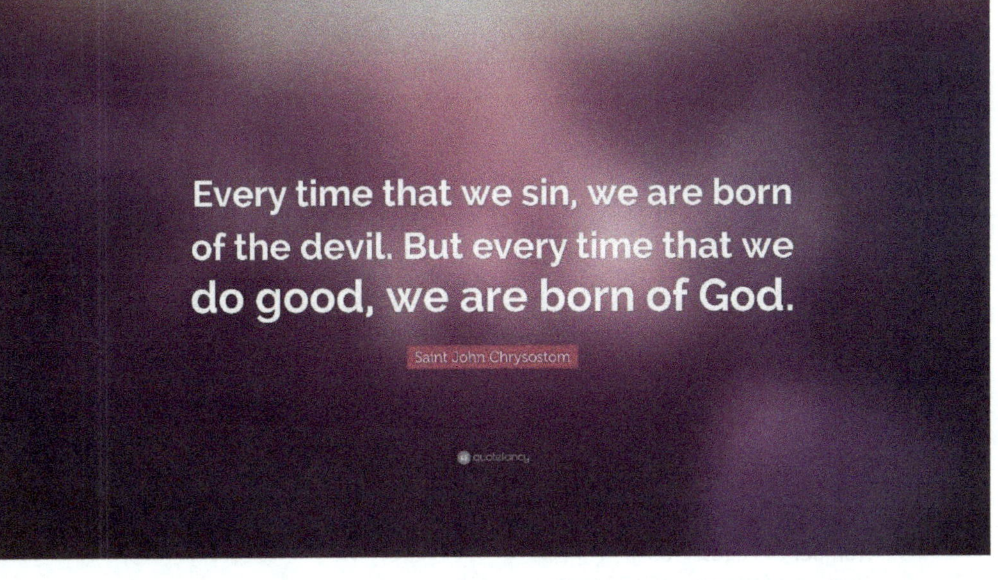
Every time that we sin, we are born of the devil. But every time that we do good, we are born of God.
Saint John Chrysostom
quotefancy

Filename: Servers Manual Christ Church.docx
Directory: C:\Users\Mark\Documents
Template:
C:\Users\Mark\AppData\Roaming\Microsoft\Templates\Normal.dot
m
Title:
Subject:
Author:
Keywords:
Comments:
Creation Date: 2022/08/17 12:31:00
Change Number: 1
Last Saved On: 2022/08/18 16:46:00
Last Saved By:
Total Editing Time: 0 Minutes
Last Printed On:
As of Last Complete Printing
Number of Pages: 83
Number of Words: 10 573 (approx.)
Number of Characters: 60 267 (approx.)

www.ingramcontent.com/pod-product-compliance
Lightning Source LLC
LaVergne TN
LVHW010358160826
845677LV00005BA/1304

* 9 7 9 8 8 4 6 9 8 6 6 7 1 *